WESTMAR COLLEGE

The Harvest of the Spirit

The Harvest of the Spirit

Reflections on Galatians 5:22

Thomas A. Langford

48-563

The Upper Room
Nashville, Tennessee

The Harvest of the Spirit

All scripture quotations, unless otherwise indicated, are from *The New English Bible,* © The Delegates of the Oxford University Press and the Syndics of the Cambridge University Press 1961 and 1970, and are reprinted by permission.

The scripture quotations designated (RSV) are from the Revised Standard Version of the Bible, copyrighted 1946, 1952, and © 1971 by the Division of Christian Education, National Council of Churches of Christ in the United States of America, and are used by permission.

The initials (KJV) are used to identify quotations from the King James Version of the Bible.

"Hymn of Joy," by Henry Van Dyke, printed by permission of Charles Scribner's Sons.

Quotation from *I Never Promised You a Rose Garden* by Hannah Green (Joanne Greenberg). Copyright ©1964 by Hannah Green. Reprinted by permission of Holt, Rinehart and Winston, Publishers.

Passage quoted from *Sixpence in Her Shoe* by Phillis McGinley (Copyright © Phyllis McGinley 1964). Permission granted by Macmillan Publishing Co., Inc.

Jean Starr Untermeyer's poem/hymn "Temper My Spirit, O Lord," reprinted by permission of Michel B. Farano, literary executor for Jean Starr Untermeyer.

First Printing, June 1981 (5)
Second Printing, April 1982 (5)
Library of Congress Catalog Card Number: 81-50602
ISBN: 0-8358-0428-3
Printed in the United States of America

"I am the real vine, and my Father is the gardener. Every barren branch of mine he cuts away; and every fruiting branch he cleans, to make it more fruitful still. You have already been cleansed by the word that I spoke to you. Dwell in me, as I in you. No branch can bear fruit by itself, but only if it remains united with the vine; no more can you bear fruit, unless you remain united with me. I am the vine, and you the branches. He who dwells in me, as I dwell in him, bears much fruit; for apart from me you can do nothing."

John 15:1-5

Contents

Preface

*"But the harvest of the Spirit is love,
joy, peace, patience, kindness,
goodness, fidelity, gentleness, and
self-control."*

Galatians 5:22-23a

In one short sentence the apostle Paul sums
up the Christian quality possible in human
life. He calls this the "harvest" or the "fruit"
of the Spirit, and he believes that these
characteristics should be realized as we come
to maturity in Jesus Christ. To reflect upon
these virtues is to be led into an awareness of
the many and rich dimensions of Christian
living. I invite you to enter into these initial
reflections and then to go beyond what is
here suggested into explorations of your own.

*The poems in this book designated AML are
by Ann Marie Langford.*

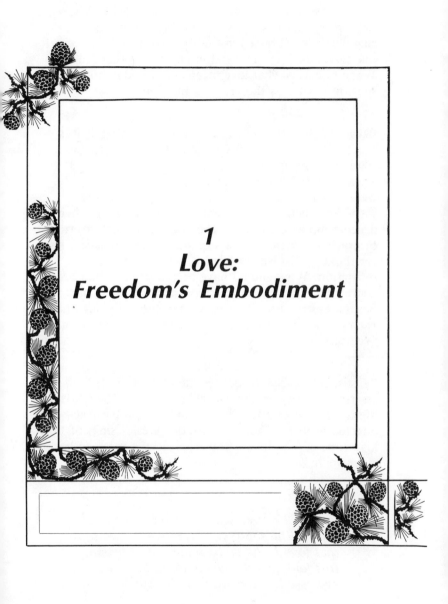

1
Love:
Freedom's Embodiment

The Harvest of the Spirit

"The harvest of the Spirit is love" (Gal. 5:22). The word *harvest* or *fruit* is singular in the Greek, and its singularity is expressed in the first word: *love*. Love is the one fruit which is expressed in all of the other fruits. When one asks what love means in everyday life, one specific answer is the fruit of the Spirit.

Before seeking to find the character of this fruit, it is necessary to understand the context of this discussion. Paul was writing to Christians who were formerly Jews. These people knew something about the good life; they were serious followers of the Torah—the law, the way—and they wanted to enhance the quality of their discipleship as Christians. The law, which had grown out of grace and which was a sustainer of graciousness, had, for these people who revered it, also become a restriction. What should have been a support had become a strait-jacket; what should have been releasing had become restricting. The law, rather than goodness, had become the chief concern. A reordering of values was necessary.

"Christ set us free, to be free men" (Gal. 5:1), Paul asserts as he begins our particular chapter. The Christian life is a new life; it is a life set upon its proper tracks, directed to its true goal. So Charles Wesley sings of "the loadstone of Thy love." But what does it mean to be emancipated?

> *How is life lived when it is set free by Jesus Christ? The short, yet complete, response is that love is the embodiment of Christian freedom, and the character of love is expressed in the fruit of the Spirit.*

It is the particular love which was expressed in Jesus
Christ to which we point: that love which was brought to
sharp focus on the cross, released with power in the
resurrection, and found in the fellowship of the church.
So unique was the expression of this love that early
Greek-speaking Christians used a relatively rare and
unknown word, *agape*, and filled it with fresh meaning
from their experience of Christ. By Christ we are set free;
in Christ we express our freedom.

*Love is freedom's embodiment. Freedom in
Christ finds its fulfillment in love, in the life
of radical self-giving to God and to neighbor.*

We speak of life and love as though they were somehow
separable, as if the latter were contained in the former.
Life and love are not separate; they are one. Life is love
in active formation. Love is no specialized compartment
of life; it is our selfhood in its most basic construction
and in its most fundamental expression. Love is life and
life is love as formed by God and shaped in conformity
with Jesus Christ. Love is the sculpting of life by the
grace of God, and it is the contouring of life through
gracious service to others.

*Love is never individualistic; to love is to live
in relation with God and other persons, to
communicate one's self to another who is
different, and to accept one's self in relation
to others.*

As life finds itself in community, so love is the most
basic expression of community; it is formed by and

forms community; love is community in its most
distinctive stance.

H. Richard Niebuhr has reminded us of four facets of
love, and here we follow his suggestions:

> *1. Love rejoices. It rejoices in the existence
> of the one who is loved; it is happy in the
> thought of him or her; it wants the presence
> of the loved one when he or she is absent.*

> *2. Love is grateful. It is thankful for the
> other; it happily accepts everything that the
> other gives without the jealous feeling that it
> ought to be able to give as much; it is
> wonder over the other's gift of herself or
> himself in companionship.*

> *3. Love is reverent. It maintains distance
> while at the same time drawing near. It does
> not wish to consume the other or want to be
> consumed by the other; rather it takes delight
> in the otherness of the other. It wants the
> other to be what he or she is and does not
> wish to remake the loved one into a model
> of itself or to use him or her as a means for
> its own advancement.*

> *4. Love is loyalty. It is the willingness to give
> one's self for the other; it desires to make the
> other what he or she can be; it is more
> willing to be destroyed than to see the other
> destroyed.[1]*

For Paul also, freedom in God means finding the ability

to mature into the man or woman each one of us was created to be; it means a growing realization of those qualities of life which bring us to full personhood in God through Jesus Christ. Such maturation is the birthright of every Christian. The fruit of the Spirit is to be found in every Christian life. Such fruiting is in contrast to the gifts of the Spirit which Paul mentions in First Corinthians 12. The gifts are possessed only by some persons; they are selectively given and have as their end the building up of the Body of Christ, the community of believers. But the fruit of the Spirit is to be characteristic of all those who are in Christ, and its chief evidence is the moral quality of life.

In love we find the shaping power of the spirit of Jesus Christ upon our spirits. Paul's list is not arbitrary. The fruit of the spirit is a description of the character of Jesus Christ, and it is a description of human character as it becomes Christlike. Read carefully Paul's larger description of love in First Corinthians 13.

> *"Love is patient and kind; love is not jealous or boastful; it is not arrogant or rude. Love does not insist on its own way; it is not irritable or resentful; it does not rejoice at wrong, but rejoices in the right. Love bears all things, believes all things, hopes all things, endures all things. Love never ends (vv. 4-8, RSV).*

> *Love is patient; love is kind and envies no one. Love is never boastful, nor conceited, nor rude; never selfish, not quick to take offense. Love keeps no score of wrongs; does not gloat over other men's sins, but delights in the truth. There is nothing love cannot*

face; there is no limit to its faith, its hope, and its endurance" (vv. 4-7).

Love is the most difficult of all qualities to discuss because it is at the same time the most basic and the most inclusive indication of character. Christians are baptized into a life which is summed up in love. All graces describing the Spirit's fruit are forms of love.

Life is an adventure in love taking flesh.

From the mystery of God's love for us we move to the life of love which is given to God. There is a holy hush over the inexplicable communion between the Creator and the creature, over the embrace of the seeking Savior and the responding believer. Yet in this mystery and miracle of love our lives are rooted.

> *Love I give in*
> *Bits and pieces*
> *Here and there,*
> *Not too much*
> *To overwhelm,*
> *For who, but God, would dare*
> *To offer all?*
>
> *AML*

The relationship between divine charity and human response is not a flight of the "alone to the Alone." There is another dimension—a necessary, undetachable dimension: the love of God carries with it the love of one's neighbor.

The relationship is tight: to love God is to love one's neighbor. The two are not identical, but they are inseparable; there cannot be one without the other (1 John 2:9-10). Love, critical love, disturbs us, judges us, and thereby redeems us. Once again, this is a mystery, for why and how we are able to love is a gift of grace; it is an achievement of God through us.

Love is corporate reality. We have overindividualized our notions of love, as though it is just a matter of one with one. But genuine love creates true community; it is enhanced by community; it includes the dimensions of community. The most adequate concrete expression of love is the existence of the Body of Christ. As Christians, we have received love; now we pray that we shall be shown how to walk in love.

Jean Troy tells of her return to China and worshiping in the newly opened Moore Memorial Church (now called Mo-en or Grace Church) in Shanghai. An old minister of some eighty years spoke to the congregation. He reminded them that the motto of their society was, "We are here to serve the people." To this he added, "If we are to be Christians in China today, we must love more than others."

Always there is the movement toward the neighbor. Shared love is a gift of grace; it occurs as God loves one person through another. For such human love is not in the last analysis really a human possibility. Authentic love knows how to forgive, to support, to accept, to endure, to rejoice, to be faithful, to go through good and bad, and to draw from and give to another. "There is nothing love cannot face" (1 Cor. 13:7); indeed, there is nothing love will not face. Such quality is not the native tendency of persons, rather it is a reflection of divine grace in human relationships.

> *Human love allows the infiltration of the Holy Spirit into human society.*

And the more a society creates real forms of love in human relationships, neighbor responsibility, justice, and peace, the more it manifests grace as love in the world.

There is mystery about love: there are depths which cannot be fathomed; there are dimensions toward which we can only tentatively point. There is also an immediate, actualized quality of love. What we may not know completely we do, nevertheless, know truly. We experience the love of God for us, and we know the wonder, amazement, and consent of worshipful response. We experience a love for our neighbor and discover what it means to care deeply for another. We are loved by a wife, a husband, a parent, a child, or a friend, and we are again amazed by grace. Such love does occur, and in its occurrence, Christian life is begun and fulfilled.

> *"Very excellent things are spoken of love; it is the essence, the spirit, the life of all virtue. It is not only the first and great command, but it is all the commandments in one."[2] "Let all you do," the apostle Paul says, "be done in love" (1 Cor. 16:14).*

The secret of love is that it opens up the whole, tangled, many-leveled reality of our personhood to the Holy

Spirit, and allows that Spirit to permeate and transform the sinews and muscles, the attitudes and affections, the sensitivities and efforts of our lives. "He who abides in love abides in God, and God abides in him" (1 John 4:16, RSV). So the Christian has "deep roots and firm foundations" in love (Eph. 3:17). But what is the evidence of the Spirit's indwelling? The chief evidence is moral character, developed sensitivity, unselfish service, and strength for doing good. It consists, in short, in the fruit of the Spirit.

Love is the truth upon which all of the other branches are grafted.

Therefore, "Put love first" (1 Cor. 14:1), for love contains the entire range of holiness. Life continues to surge from God, and fruit begins to mature.

A New Testament prayer draws all of this together: Paul prays that God "out of the treasures of his glory . . . may grant you strength and power through his Spirit in your inner being, that . . . you be strong to grasp, with all God's people, what is the breadth and length and height and depth of the love of Christ. . . . So may you attain to the fullness . . . of God himself" (Eph. 3:16-19).

We must not fear
To touch another's need,
To show we care,
To spin a web,
To be a clasp and anchor
To each other, Lord,
Within the fold of thy most tender love.
                                        AML

19

2
Joy:
Love Released
for Loving

The Harvest of the Spirit

The fruit of the Spirit is real fruit; that is, it embodies seeds which may be planted and which bring new growth, but there must be planting for fruit to be realized. This is the case with joy. Joy is known in the sharing of life; it is a way of life in relation to others.

> *Joy is love released for loving. It is a delight about life, a delight in sharing life, a delight expressed in living. Joy arises from being loved and loving.*

In the baptism of infants, often we pray that the child may be led into "that life of faith whose strength is righteousness and whose fruit is everlasting joy and peace." We begin Christian life with a hope for joy.

The quality of joy is difficult to capture; the deepest dimensions of life are always difficult to bring to language. This is especially true of joy, for joy refers to a wholeness of life, a sense of the good meaning which permeates our attitudes and actions.

> *Joy is love reaching to the nerve ends of life.*

We must allow for the range of joy. Human life is varied and is expressed in a variety of ways, so joy comes to different lives in different guises. Joy does not mean always being on top; we can't sing high C all of the time. Nor does joy mean simply laughter or health or adequate goods. Life filled by the presence of God, in whatever circumstances, is joyful; this may come through laughter or tears, health or illness, adequate or inadequate conditions in external life. "With joy," Isaiah says,

"shall ye draw water out of the wells of salvation"
(12:3, KJV).

At its center, however, joy is simple; it is an immediate
relating to life. Joy is spontaneous. It has a genius for
embracing ordinary events. It takes life as it comes and
then overcomes life.

> *Joy is a pure sense of life; it is filled time, an
> unconsciousness about time.*

Never found by direct seeking, joy is a gift. We
experience joy when we are so engaged that we fail to
ask if we are joyful, such as when we read a good book,
visit with a friend, or play a game and then discover it is
an hour later than we thought. To understand this
dimension of life, we need a clock that measures not only
the passing of time but the quality of time passed. "In
thy presence is the fullness of joy" (Psalm 16:11).

> *Joy is creative. It finds its life by giving its
> life.*

There is in joy a profound unselfconsciousness—an
awareness of surroundings, of persons, of happenings.
There is embrace, a willingness to see value, a desire to
relate to those realities. So William Blake writes in
"Eternity":

> *"He who binds to himself a Joy
> Doth the wingéd life destroy."*

The Harvest of the Spirit

Joy, Christian joy, is a fruit of the Spirit, not the
gratification of our emotions; joy opens us to the deepest
meanings of life. The writer of First John puts the matter
in direct language. "What we have seen and heard we
declare to you, so that you and we together may share in
a common life, that life which we share with the Father
and his Son Jesus Christ. And we write this in order that
the joy of us all may be complete" (1:3-4). So Saint
Irenaeus, a second-century Christian, claimed that the
glory of God is a vital, fully alive person.

Another early Christian, Saint Augustine, writes of
happiness with his persistent logic.

> *"The title happy cannot, in my opinion,
> belong either to him who has not what he
> loves, whatever it may be, or to him who has
> what he loves if it is hurtful, or to him who
> does not love what he has, although it is
> good in perfection. . . . The happy life exists
> . . . when that which is man's chief good is
> both loved and possessed."*[1]

The experience of joy requires some discuncing from
one's self; it is a freedom from ourselves and our own
small, artifically-limited world. Among human beings,
saints soar because they think lightly of themselves. So
joy comes from large vision, from a vision of far
horizons. It sees life in its true dimensions. It lives under
God.

Joy reflects a relaxed sense about one's own life; it
moves with the freedom found only in those who are
uncalculating. Michael Kaufman has commented that in
Mother Teresa, who has worked in the slums of
Calcutta, human clay is molded in unambiguous joy.

24

Now, back to our beginning point.

*Joy is a fruit of the Spirit; it is experienced as
life is released by God and released to God.*

But joy is of the Spirit. It is not merely a titillation of
our emotions. It is not the same as what we usually call
happiness; it is far deeper than that, for joy is the welling
up of the presence of God in human life. There is a great
emotional range to joy among persons or within one life,
but the range comes from the one source, God.

*"Thou art giving and forgiving,
Ever blessing, ever blest,
Well-spring of the joy of living,
Ocean depth of happy rest!
Thou our Father, Christ our Brother—
All who live in love are Thine:
Teach us how to love each other,
Lift us to the Joy Divine."
Henry Van Dyke, "Hymn of Joy"*

Again, such joy is known only in sharing. There must be
a planting for fruit to be born. And joy is fruitful; it is a
seed-bearing fruit which finds its life in the life it gives.
Joy is not containable within the narrow limits of one life
alone; it breaks the boundaries of self-interest and self-
concern. Joy expresses community and ricochets with
abandon through community.

The sharing of joy is the sharing of a total life in a total
way with others. There is no calculation in this
giving—joy is not even shared to make others happy or

joyful. It is shared because it is its nature to share.

> *Joy spreads—whether by soft ripples or wild cascades—over the lives of others. Joy, therefore, is a corporate and incorporating reality. It is found in relationships rather than in solitariness. Joy is never a private possession. It is a shared and sharing reality.*

But is this a type of pious hope which is not actually achieved in ordinary human life? Sometimes we speak of Christian life as though it is not a dimension of our usual course of activity; we have allowed it to become separated, placed in a special setting, held for a particular part of the week, allowed to operate only within approved arenas. But joy upsets these careful restraints; it refuses such limitations. Joy is completeness promising more completeness.

Jesus, in the Gospel of John, speaks of the "more abundant" life; there is the expectation that his followers will experience this quality of living. Indeed, the more abundance which Jesus offers is actually experienced by his followers. This is our promise and possibility.

I have watched people lose their joy in searches for truth, for power, and for meaning. Many years ago I had a friend—a capable, energetic, ambitious young man. He moved through life seeking and gaining many things, but he commented to me late in his pilgrimage: "I somewhere lost my joy." We seek joy so desperately and miss our goal so completely. This man lost his joy and tenaciously sought to regain it. But his search for joy was always frustrated, for joy is a gift. It does not come at the end of a search.

*Joy is a fulfillment of life effected by the
Spirit of God; it is found in the sharing of
life. Joy is a by-product; it is a spontaneous
fruit of the Spirit. As a fruiting of God in
human life, it cannot be forced or demanded.*

The expression of joy may be in weeping or laughter; it is
the positive release of life to the well-being God gives.
W. E. Sangster, the English Methodist preacher of the
last generation, wrote ten new commandments for
Christians.

*"1. Thou shalt enjoy this lovely world which
God has made: sun, moon, and stars; fields,
flowers, and trees; wind, warmth, and rain;
earth, sea and sky.
2. Thou shalt enjoy the gift of love from
parents, sweetheart, wife, the love which
goes on loving when you are most unlovely.
3. Thou shalt enjoy home—where you do not
visit but belong; where your absence means a
gap which no one else can fill.
4. Thou shalt enjoy the trustfulness of little
children and their adoring belief that there is
nothing you do not know and nothing you
cannot do.
5. Thou shalt enjoy friends, their loyalty and
fellowship, their constancy in sorrow, and
their unprotesting acceptance of your timely
help.
6. Thou shalt enjoy wholesome laughter, the
ludicrous incident, the side-splitting joke.
7. Thou shalt enjoy art, music, the cinema,
literature, eloquence, animals, singing,
rhythm, games.*

> 8. *Thou shalt enjoy the privilege of helping others: the poor and sick, the aged and maimed.*
> 9. *Thou shalt enjoy peace. This peace shall not attach only to your circumstances: it shall abide in your heart.*
> 10. *Thou shalt enjoy God; the knowledge that He is there and that He is love; that He cares for all.*[2]

Joy persists through good and bad. It does not exist without a sense of the tragic, but it moves through the surface of life to basic foundations. Joseph Addison says in "An Hymn,"

> *"Ten Thousand thousand precious gifts*
> *my daily thanks employ;*
> *nor is the least a cheerful heart*
> *that tastes those gifts with joy."*

Nehemiah 8:10 says, "Joy in the Lord is your strength," and we pray, "Restore to [us] the joy of thy salvation" (Psalm 51:12, RSV).

> *The sun begins to dance*
> *On rippled water*
> *When the summer's done.*
> *Floors need sweeping,*
> *Fires need laying,*
> *Dirty dishes wait while I*
> *Watch the sunlight dance on water*
> *And revel in its fire.*
>
> *AML*

3
Peace:
Love Expressing
Its Depth

Peace is love expressing its depth. The source of peace is the life of God. "He is himself our peace" (Eph. 2:14), the New Testament affirms. This internal peace exists quite apart from external circumstances; indeed it is especially noticeable when it is expressed in the midst of challenging and negating surroundings.

External conditions of life do not produce peace. At one extreme, we sometimes yearn for ideal circumstances and think such a situation will produce peace. On this end of the spectrum, Ludwig Wittgenstein has commented that since on ice there is no friction, in a certain sense the conditions are ideal. However, precisely because of that, we are unable to walk. At the other extreme, negative circumstances do not necessarily create character even though character may be developed within and in relation to negative circumstances. Character may be either destroyed or built up by negative reality.

> *Peace is reconciliation and fresh conciliation. It creates a climate of acceptance. Peace reaches the most radical depths so that a sense of the eternal becomes the gyroscope of human living. With this center, we are ready for anything because we are rooted in eternity.*

In one sense, peace is always won at great price. It is, in the Christian tradition, linked to the cross. Consequently, God's peace is won through God's sufferings, and our peace is found in God in the midst of cruciform possibility. But this notion runs against our hopes. As James Martineau writes:

Peace: Love Expressing Its Depth

"The first impulse of 'the natural man' is to seek peace by mending his external condition; to quiet desire by increase of ease, to banish anxiety by increase of wealth, to guard against hostility by making himself too strong for it; to build up his life into a fortress of security and a palace of comfort. . . . The spirit of Christianity casts away at once this whole theory of peace."[3]

Christian peace comes from trust in God. Peace is a quality of life which undergirds and is expressed through other dimensions.

Karen moved from Atlanta to a new home. She sat down and made a list of needs and hopes: a new craft, baking, a community, a job through which she could serve, intentional reading . . . and peace. Later she discovered that she had found peace through the other things she did. Peace is not an isolated part of life; it is a dimension of experience which is found in and with our activities.

A man whose mother recently died described to me his mother's reaction to her impending death. "How do you feel?" he asked. "Are you afraid?" She replied, "I am afraid, but I am not worried." That is a clear witness to peace, for a peaceful spirit is able to look reality in the eye; it does not demand or pretend that reality is other than it is. In facing the actual conditions, one is wise to recognize their destructive ability and to be respectfully frightened. But even in the midst of honest and poignant fear, there is, in the deepest reservoir of our spirit, a still, cool, unworried point. It is that point where the stillness of God creates a quietness in our lives.

An unusual compliment was paid by a six-year-old girl to a neighbor. The girl and her two brothers often went to the neighbor's home to play. When asked why they enjoyed playing in that home, she replied, "Because even when it's noisy, it is always quiet." This is the gift of peace.

The word *peace* has two classical meanings. In Greek it means harmony, the proper and beautiful balancing of all things; it is found in the harmony of the spheres. In Hebrew peace or *shalom* stands for well-being. (This word is so difficult to translate that twenty-four Greek words are used for it in the Septuagint). In both instances the word carries a sense of wholeness, completeness, rich fulfillment; it is tranquility of order based on justice.

In the letter to the Ephesians, Paul is commenting on the long enmity between the Gentiles and the Jews. In Christ, he claims, this seemingly bottomless rift has been healed. The chasm has been bridged, for Jesus Christ has created "out of the two a single new humanity in himself, thereby making peace" (Eph. 2:15).

> *To experience peace is to share peace; peace must issue into peacemaking. Peace is a quality of life and a quality of shared life. The deep inner quality projects itself into external conditions; a profound personal quality carries public responsibility.*

Yet peace has been an elusive hope in human history. While there is great value in personal peace, there is special responsibility for the achievement of world peace. "Blessed are the peacemakers," Jesus said (Matt. 5:9, KJV). Christian statesmanship and Christian servanthood come to special significance as peace among human beings is actually achieved. We stand before the possibility of Armageddon; our lives are crossed with the shadow of nuclear destruction. In this context, we are called to serve the cause of peace. We are charged with the responsibility of making peace, if we are to see our world survive. We are to extend the peace of God.

Peace may be falsely served. Jeremiah speaks against those who cry, " 'Peace, peace,' when there is no peace" (Jer. 6:14, 8:11, RSV). We as followers of the Messiah Jesus are to seek genuine peace. Counterfeit peace will not do. Genuine peace is often found only through directly facing evil with the innovative resourcefulness of Spirit-guided living.

In Romans, Paul draws several virtues into interesting juxtaposition. "For the kingdom of God is not eating and drinking, but justice, peace, and joy, inspired by the Holy Spirit" (14:17). Look at the qualities mentioned: justice, peace, and joy. In the Christian life these virtues are found together: the service of justice is the expression of peace and joy; peace is sought through justice and issues in joy; joy is embodied in justice and peace. The Christian life is whole; the fruits of the Spirit grow on the same stem.

> *Peace is not anesthesia. It is not a hope for the future which forgets the present. Peace is experienced in the midst of this life. It is trust in God when situations are difficult. It is a broadening of feeling, a deepening of insight into the meaning of life. Peace has to do, not with the foam of the waves, but with the deep reaches of the ocean.*

Karl Rahner, a Roman Catholic theologian, has put the

issue into a similar frame of reference. What we know, he says, "is only a small island in a vast sea that has not been traveled. It is a floating island, and it might be more familiar to us than the sea, but ultimately it is borne by the sea and only because it is can we be borne by it."[2]

Peace comes when we realize that "the eternal God is [our] refuge, and underneath are the everlasting arms" (Deut. 33:27, KJV). To say this in a slightly different way, it is only when the whole thrust of our being is reordered by God and set towards God that peace is established in our lives. Peace is a gift; it is the gift of the attracting presence of God. "Thou wilt keep him in perfect peace, whose mind is stayed on thee" (Isa. 26:3, KJV).

Washington Gladden put the right words into his hymn "O Master, Let Me Walk with Thee":

> *"In peace that only thou canst give,*
> *With thee, O Master, let me live."*

There is an appropriateness to the prayer of Paul:

> *"And may the God of hope fill you with all*
> *joy and peace by your faith in him, until, by*
> *the power of the Holy Spirit, you overflow*
> *with hope."* Romans 15:13

The fruits of the Spirit are undivided. Where love and joy and peace are not found, there will be no production of gentleness, kindness, or temperance. The fruits are clustered together.

Peace: Love Expressing Its Depth

"Let us then pursue the things that make for peace."   Romans 14:19

> Peace is
>> To pass beneath a canopy
>> Of bare branched trees and
>> See the blue of sky beyond
>> To feel the clarity
>> Of winter's chill
>> And be aware
>> That spring will come.

AML

4
Patience:
Love Enduring
Over Time

The Harvest of the Spirit

The most patient man I have known always prayed for patience. It is strange, but perhaps important, that one sometimes lives better than one knows; the qualities of life which one takes to be of basic significance are often revealed in one's actual living.

Patience is primary as a way of relating to God and with other persons. In relation to God, patience is closely associated with a sense of providence. Patience represents the capacity to wait for God's will to show itself in the situation and to share in God's long-range purposes. To be patient is to have a large view; it is to have the horizons of one's experience expanded so that one is able to set immediate circumstances into the extended perspective of God.

It is significant that persons who are sick are called patients, that is, those who wait for the process of healing or dying. Such processes move at their own pace. They require that we move into the natural rhythms and tides of life. To be a good patient is to have patience; it is to wait trustingly with God.

Long-suffering on the part of the Christian is a response to the long-suffering quality of God. For it is God who is patient beyond all expectation. It is God whose love is steadfast, unfailing, infinitely tender, and continually nurturing our spirits. It is the patient love of God which calls us to be patient before God and with others.

Patience is to be expressed in our relation with other persons. Patience is positive. It sees other persons as gifts. It is a recognition of the integrity of others, of their own distinctive personhood, of the validity of their pulsations and modes of maturation. Patience allows and supports the development of others in the ways which are authentic for them.

"Do you not know, have you not heard?
The Lord, the everlasting God, creator of the
*   wide world,*
*   grows neither weary nor faint;*
*   no man can fathom his understanding.*
He gives vigour to the weary,
new strength to the exhausted.
Young men may grow weary and faint,
even in their prime they may stumble and
fall;
but those who look to the Lord will win new
*   strength,*
they will grow wings like eagles;
they will run and not be weary,
they will march on and never grow faint."
                                        Isaiah 40:28-31

Margery Williams, in *The Velveteen Rabbit,* tells of
stuffed animals in a playroom talking.

> *" 'What is REAL?' asked the Rabbit one*
> *day. . . . 'Does it mean having things that*
> *buzz inside you and a stick-out handle?'*
>
> *'Real isn't how you are made,' said the Skin*
> *Horse. 'It's a thing that happens to you.*
> *When a child loves you for a long, long time,*
> *not just to play with, but REALLY loves you,*
> *then you become real.'. . .*
>
> *'It doesn't happen all at once. . . . You*
> *become. It takes a long time. . . . Generally,*
> *by the time you are Real, most of your hair*
> *has been loved off, and your eyes drop out*

and you get loose in the joints and very
shabby. But these things don't matter at all,
because once you are Real you can't be ugly,
except to people who don't understand.' "[1]

The apostle Paul puts it plainly, "Love is patient"
(1 Cor. 13:4). For patience is love in its persistent
posture—love which refuses to be disloyal, unsteady, or
erratic.

Patience and maturity are closely interrelated. Hurry and
impatience are always the mark of the amateur; the
accomplished worker or artist, the mature person, knows
how to allow the distinctive quality to come of its own
accord. Patience before God means that one is ready to
move at God's pace, to speed up or slow down, to do or
wait according to the timing of God. Patience is allowing
fruit to come in its season; it is waiting for things to
reach their time.

> *"My times are in Thy hand:*
> *My God, I wish them there."*
> *William F. Lloyd*

Growth requires sun and wind and rain. Maturation does
not take place with even-cadenced, equal-length steps.
Rather it knows the challenge of the storm, the lack of
nutrients, the period of drought as well as the fresh rain,
the warm sun, and the new shoot. Hannah Green, in *I
Never Promised You a Rose Garden*, tells a poignant
story of a girl named Deborah.

"Her dream began with winter darkness. Out
of this darkness came a great hand, fisted. It
was a man's hand, powerful and hollowed by

shadows in the wells between bones and
tendons. The fist opened and in the long
plain of the palm lay three small pieces of
coal. Slowly the hand closed, causing within
the fist a tremendous pressure. The pressure
began to generate a white heat and still it
increased. There was a sense of weighing,
crushing time. She seemed to feel the
suffering of the coal with her own body,
almost beyond the point of being borne. At
last she cried out to the hand, 'Stop it! Will
you never end it! Even a stone cannot bear
to this limit . . . even a stone . . . !'

After what seemed like too long a time for
anything molecular to endure, the torments
in the fist relaxed. The fist turned slowly and
very slowly opened.

Diamonds, three of them.

Three clear and brilliant diamonds, shot with
light, lay in the good palm. A deep voice
called to her, 'Deborah!' and then, gently,
'Deborah, this will be you.' '[2]

These things I know:
The wind will blow,
The rain will come,
The sun will shine again,
   and so will I—
   by God's enduring grace.
Blows the wind
   before the rain;
Rainbows promise
   sun again
     in time.   *AML*

The Harvest of the Spirit

Patience is the capacity to wait for God's will to show itself in a particular situation. There is no demand that the circumstances conform to our own hopes or comfort or ease; rather, there is a readiness to accept the conditions under which we must live, even as we persistently seek to do God's will in the situation. Patience in the world is a readiness for God; there is no sanctioning of evil or injustice or meanness. Rather, with patience we bend our backs to service in the world; we persistently go forward to challenge the world; we work with tenacity for change in our world.

In so much of life the conditions are given. The questions for us are: How shall we respond? What shall we make of the situation in which we are placed?

It is not patience to allow what exists merely to continue. Rather, patience for others is readiness to wait for, while also gently encouraging, those others. Patience is standing resolutely for a new order of things. Patience serves goodness; it is waiting for God. Consequently, patience is not to be separated from the goal of love. So Jesus instructs his disciples: "As you go proclaim the message: 'The Kingdom of Heaven is upon you.' Heal the sick,raise the dead, cleanse lepers, cast out devils. You received without cost; give without charge" (Matt. 10:7-8).

The goal we seek is the well-being of others, so patience is enduring with positive intention. To heal the brokeness of our world, to draw together that which is sundered, to renew relationships, to seek justice, to walk with determination toward long-range goals—all of this is the expression of Christian patience. Such patience always works under the awareness of the large charity of God.

Jesus says, "In your patience possess ye your souls" (Luke 21:19, KJV). He was speaking to an anxious people, people who doubted God's providence and who were anxious about survival. Yet patience was more basic, for patience is a witness to the ability to trust one's life to God; it is paced movement, not frantic activity.

> *Refuse to mourn*
> *The season's end;*
> *Accept the change;*
> *Leave passing time,*
> *What is to come,*
> *In my Master's hand.*
> *AML*

To possess patience is to be able to maintain an easy graciousness in the midst of fatiguing moments, to hold on without great show of holding on. Patience is long-suffering. It is identification with other persons over time without becoming cynical or exhausted; it is to suffer without allowing the suffering to parade itself.

To be patient does not mean to have no temper. It is positive; it means to have a good temper. It is to possess the caring which seeks others' good in ways which are most beneficial for the other persons. Patience is having time for other persons, and it means caring for society's good in ways which are most beneficial for the social order.

Life is paced by God. To have patience is to

43

> move at God's pace; it is to move in rhythm
> with the rhythm of God's gracious love.
> "Never," Oswald Chambers cautions, "run
> before God's guidance."[3]

God's patience draws the disparate dimensions of our
lives quietly and steadily toward their appointed end.
Therefore Jesus enjoins us, "Bring forth fruit with
patience" (Luke 8:15, KJV).

John Wesley's covenant prayer draws many of these
themes together.

> "I am no longer my own, but thine. Put me
> to what thou wilt, rank me with whom thou
> wilt; put me to doing, put me to suffering; let
> me be employed for thee or laid aside for
> thee, exalted for thee or brought low for
> thee; let me be full, let me be empty; let me
> have all things, let me have nothing; I freely
> and heartily yield all things to thy pleasure
> and disposal. . . . Amen."

5
Kindness:
Love as Thoughtfulness

The Harvest of the Spirit

Kindness, loving kindness, is characteristic of God's relation to persons. "With lovingkindness have I drawn thee," Jeremiah says, speaking for God (Jer. 31:3, KJV). This is God's way of coming to us in Jesus Christ, and it is to be characteristic of Christian living.

Kindness is gracious accommodation to others; it represents an attitude, a style, and a way of being in life. Kindness is a double gift: ability to help another, while not injuring the other's self-respect. The quality of kindness is dependent upon the character of a person; it is a loving expression of one sensitive spirit touching another. On this, the hymn to love in First Corinthians 13 is direct: "Love is kind" (verse 4).

> *Kindness is love as thoughtfulness; it is consideration of others. Kindness also possesses a firmness which moves across the contours of another life with a shaping touch that brings out the natural grain and distinctive form that was given to that life in creation.*

This character of love is provided for Christian life by the character of God's love. Divine charity gives us our true humanity; it is active in bringing out the intentions for life which were present in creation but spoiled by human sinfulness. Redeeming love reforms the lost image of a person's original creation.

> *"Let us with a gladsome mind*
> *Praise the Lord, for he is kind*

For his mercies aye endure,
Ever faithful, ever sure."
                    John Milton,
                    based on Psalm 136

There is about kindness an obliviousness to self, for
kindness represents a passage beyond self-defensiveness.
Such virtue expresses itself in action as an ability to give
to other persons without detracting from their special
gifts or abilities.

> *Kindness is the opposite of manipulation; it is*
> *love which gives without incurring debts.*

It is easier to give when we are honored for the giving;
yet too often, self-importance spoils service. We reinforce
our pride in the guise of doing good. But kindness is love
which gives without pride; it knows how to offer its
concern so that it may be most easily and helpfully
accepted. Kindness carries a willingness to be frugal with
oneself so that everyone else may be filled.

Rita Snowden tells a story of Alice Freeman Palmer, a
beloved principal of Wellesley College who died at age
forty-seven. "Mrs. Palmer, " wrote one of her former
students, "had a strange effect on me. When I saw her, I
felt as if I could do things that I never dreamed of
before. Even now, whenever I think of her, I have a
sense of dignity in life."[1] This is the way kindness affects
other persons.

At its base, kindness is a simple, everyday sort of virtue.
It is not spectacular, not showy. Kindness is by its very

nature persistent, steady, untiring concern for the other's need. Kindness is persistent thoughtfulness.

It is so easy, and so distracting, to imagine ourselves doing great things, making important speeches, being at significant places. Even in the spiritual realm, we imagine ourselves doing important, noticeable things for God. By such imaginings, we often overlook immediate possibilities. We cast our eyes to distant triumphs and miss seeing the next step, the next person, the next opportunity.

> *Kindness is the morality of the next encounter; it represents the sensitive touch which makes ordinary experience special.*

Kindness has a special place in the repertory of Christian action. It provides a track on which many of the other, more prominent qualities can travel. Kindness is the common ground upon which uncommon quality may be built. The quality of living is enhanced as kindness becomes the regular mode of relating to one another.

The late Flannery O'Connor, a fiction writer from Georgia, thought her life uninteresting because she lived it "between the house and the chicken yard."[2] But few recent novelists have known more about the radical dimensions of grace in human life. She lived in a restricted arena, due largely to physical disease, but she possessed an expansive spirit and she lived deeply. The meaning of life is found—if it is found at all—where life is actually lived, and that may well be between the house and the chicken yard.

> *To help the hurt, Not knowing other ways.*

Young arms encircle
An autistic child
Whose haunting cry goes on . . . and on.

Another day,
The one who cared
Has cause to cry,
Autistic hands reach out
To touch,
For healing has begun.

AML

Often the biography of a good person is much more
difficult to write than that of one whose life has been
infected with evil. It seems that goodness is simply not as
interesting or titillating as evil; goodness is not as
provocative or arousing as evil. Realizing this, we need to
learn how to present and how to hear accounts of
goodness.

But let us see how easily we can overlook kindness. For
instance, good manners may be an expression of
morality. Manners, of course, may be simply mannerism;
they may be superficial and even self-serving. But good
manners may and should express deeper levels of
consideration for others. As Phyllis McGinley writes:

"Charity is one traditional virtue the modern
world is willing to applaud. But what a lot we
talk about it these days, and how often we
miss its implications. Charity is not simply a
donation to the community chest and a gift
to the Hundred Neediest Cases at
Christmastime. It is not merely giving one's
hours as a volunteer in a hospital or
subscribing to the relief of flood victims a

> hemisphere away. It is both larger and
> smaller than those things, at once easier and
> harder, and it does, indeed, begin at home.
> Charity is graciousness and tact. Charity is a
> guarded tongue. It is picking up one's toys,
> giving a hand with the dinner dishes, writing
> a bread-and-butter letter to one's hostess. It is
> turning off television at a respectable hour so
> one's neighbor can sleep in peace, and being
> patient with bores. It is thanking salesladies
> in shops, forbearing to pass on the bit of
> malicious gossip so tempting to tell, wielding
> knife and fork so that we do not aesthetically
> offend."[3]

The ordinary diaries of our lives are the accounts of our spiritual living. The ordinary things we do from hour to hour are the important services of love. A minister friend says that his father was always insistent upon kindness. He would not tolerate insensitivity or callousness. His father said that kindness was the beginning part of loving somebody.[4]

John, while in high school, took a job on a farm in Ohio. He had to help with the vegetable garden and through the summer grumbled often because the garden was obviously much larger than it needed to be for the family. Only later did he learn that for years the farmwife had also fed several other families. He accepted the garden as a way of helping those for whom God cares.

Kindness involves a generosity of attitude and action; it reflects a willingness to go out of one's way—a long way out of one's way—for another person. Kindness is opposed to tit for tat; it does not measure in equal parts what is received and what is given. As with God, Christian kindness cares more for the other than it desires to be cared for by the other.

As with the other virtues, kindness is nurtured by community. It is the church which is often the nurturer of these fruits, and it is the concrete community of Christians which affirms our growth and calls us to live more fully in the Spirit. And once again we hear a word from one who is in that company of witnesses. "Put on . . . kindness" (Col. 3:12).

> *Put on kindness;*
> *Wear it faithfully*
> *To be fruitful*
> *In the knowledge of my love,*
> *Expecting no rewards.*
> *Love, do good and lend,*
> *Draw others to me,*
> *As in loving kindness*
> *I have drawn you to myself.*
> *AML*

6
Goodness:
Love Going Bone Deep

The Harvest of the Spirit

The apostle Paul sets the stage: "We pray that you may bear fruit in active goodness" (Col. 1:10). A fruit of the Spirit is goodness, and it is a worthy prayer that this harvest occur in our lives. But once again our question is, What is goodness?

Goodness is love going bone deep. The power and source of Christian life is good; its origin is God's goodness in Jesus Christ. Because God is good, human living can express goodness which is created, sustained, and cultivated by God's Spirit.

Goodness is found in a life that is thoroughly permeated by love; it is found in the transparency of life, in the same quality which goes through all of our personhood. "There must be no limit to your goodness," Jesus said, "as your heavenly Father's goodness knows no bounds" (Matt. 5:48).

But one must look with care and patience not to be deceived. Some pious people are all sheen with no substance. A character in Jane Austen's *Pride and Prejudice* remarks, "There certainly was some great mismanagement in the education of those two young men. One has got all the goodness, and the other all the appearance of it."[1]

> *Goodness is a quality of life in its own terms and a quality of life in relating to others. Being as good as the next person is not the same as being Christian. Christian goodness is godliness. In interior life, goodness represents authenticity. In relation to others, goodness has the capacity to give through genuine concern for others; it seeks the well-being of others, not its own interest.*

Dorothy Parker, in some remarks on Isadora Duncan,
the dancer, comments, "Well, there are always those
who cannot distinguish between glitter and glamour, just
as there are always those who cannot understand why
you should desire real pearls when they can't be told
from the imitations. But you can, you see, tell them from
the imitations. The neat surfaces of the imitations shine
prettily; the real glow from within."[2]

> *Last Autumn's burnished leaves*
> *Lie rotting underneath*
> *The dogwood's airy innocence*
> *As witness to eternity*
> *and God's intended good for us.*
> *AML*

The presence of the Holy Spirit in human life challenges
all that is poor, shoddy, and pretentious. It possesses the
power to transform life by weaving the different threads
of personality into good material—that is, real, hard-
wearing, solid stuff. Goodness is the gaberdine of
Christian living. A couple in rural North Carolina lived
frugally so that they could help young people through
school. They always lived in an extremely modest home.
They were careful with their resources, but they made it
possible for one or two students each year to attend
college.

One of the most starkly evident characteristics of being
good is simplicity. Goodness is simple. An old Shaker
hymn announces, " 'Tis a gift to be simple." Simple
living for God is the foundation of Christian goodness.
Goodness is what it is; it is what it is thoroughly,
consistently, and consequently without flamboyance or

self-display. Sometimes the depth which goodness possesses gives a remarkable quietness to life. Sometimes the unawareness of self that goodness has makes for robustness and outgoingness.

God is good, and Paul calls us to express the "riches of his goodness" (Rom. 2:4, KJV). There is no stereotype of goodness. It is not goody-goody or piously good or even quietly good or robustly good. Goodness sets its own stamp in a way which is appropriate to a particular person. Goodness allows for a life to express itself as it was created to be by God and with God. Goodness is the Spirit of God refracted through the diversity of human spirits.

God's grace is continuously working on the recalcitrant material of actual human character, making it supple to God's Spirit, helping persons to find their own strength and muscles. Goodness reflects God's working in the most tender and firm way with the material of our lives. There is no miserliness in goodness. Bigots are religious savages. Openness and listening and loving are expressions of goodness.

> As Colin Morris has written, "goodness involves risk and exposure because the good cannot employ the strategies of darkness used ruthlessly by the wicked for self-protection."[3]

The supreme example of goodness is Jesus Christ. "For the same God who said, 'Out of darkness let light shine', has caused his light to shine within us, to give the light of revelation—the revelation of the glory of God in the face of Jesus Christ" (2 Cor. 4:6). "You know about Jesus of

Nazareth," Peter said, "how God anointed him with the Holy Spirit and with power. He went about doing good" (Acts 10:38).

> *It is through goodness that Jesus is active and operative in the world. The fruiting of life moves outward and is active.*

Goodness is not just a soft virtue; it does not stay within itself. Goodness is strength in the service of God; it is the power of God expressed as graciousness. The expectations of our discipleship are set high. "I should wish you to be experts in goodness," Paul says, "but simpletons in evil" (Rom. 16:20).

Jesus put it plainly, "A good tree always yields good fruit" (Matt. 7:17). What is the character of the life which bears fruit? Many Christians live lives that resemble gnarled, weather-beaten, even stunted trees; others seem to be protected and well proportioned. Some lives are bent by prevailing pressure; others are straight. But all may bear fruit.

There is no single type of life which comes to harvest. Fruit may come from a life which has a rich or a limited context. Saints come in an astonishing variety of personal styles. Some persons live largely alone; some live in orchards which are rather well cared for; a few live in hothouses. Most have survived through good weather and bad, through drought and wet seasons. Fruit which comes in bumper years is good, and fruit which comes after a bad season may be valued even more.

The popular presentation of Christians as the successful people, and the pernicious presumption that to be a "real Christian" means that one finds the goods of life, is to confuse one's own well-being with the mission of God.

The Harvest of the Spirit

Christian life is conforming to Jesus Christ; it is shaped along the hard grain of the cross. The good tree does not refer to physical appearance or to that tree which has received the most favorable soil in which to grow or to that tree which has received the most attention. Goodness has to do with being well planted, with ability to survive; it has to do with the production of some abundance to be shared. Fruit is produced to be shared; abundant harvest carries seed for the beginning of new life.

"Every time is the right time to do good," says a successful business woman who now lives in a retirement home. She has experienced a wide range of life and has faced debilitating personal tragedies. Some of the most helpful words spoken to her of things done for her, she says, have come from people who just happened to think about calling or visiting and did it. Goodness claims every moment for significant meaning.

> *Goodness allows the essential vitality of life to course through us and make us productive for useful purposes. Yet such expression can be frustrated as spiritual resources are diverted or hoarded.*

Jacques Cousteau, the French explorer, has said that the building of the Aswan Dam in Egypt has prevented even one drop of water from above the dam from reaching the Mediterranean Sea. The most productive areas bordering the river are becoming unproductive as salt water from the sea pushes into the Nile. Moreover, Lake Nasser, the body of water which the dam has created, is destroying the old Nubian buildings of great antiquity. This story parallels human life, for at times we block the flow of the spirit of goodness, annulling both past meaning and future growth.

Let me tell you of two persons. Charles Kuralt once implied on his show that people called "Charlie" are never respected. But one man named Charlie is a man to respect, for he is a good man. He is open, relaxed, quick to give a hug. His daily truck route takes him over the mountains, a connector of three towns. On each day as he goes out, he stops to help a crippled owner of a fruit stand put out his display. Each day as he returns, he stops to help put the display inside. Not until years passed did some of his closest friends know of this. Then one commented with understanding, "It is typical of Charlie."

A hairdresser has for years taken off one afternoon a week to visit people who are unable to get out. She often takes with her the things she knows the friends would like to read or eat. This role has been a ritual of her life, and always it has been done with unselfconscious interest in those she visited.

Yet goodness is so often not expressed by Christians. Christians have often denied their own character through war, exploitation, manipulation, and insensitivity. Through the Holocaust to Auschwitz and today in America, Christians have denied the good they profess. Christians should not perpetrate evil; good people should do good.

In writing to the Romans, Paul says with confidence, "I have no doubt . . . that you . . . are quite full of goodness" (15:14). Yet we live poverty-stricken in the midst of spiritual richness; we are shriveled selves. How can the vital life of the Spirit be released in our lives? This remains a basic question for Christians, and the

59

answer comes only with the release of life to God. We are opened by, and must be constantly open to, the influx of the Holy Spirit. Only when we are grafted into the true vine can we bring forth good fruit.

"Thou art good and thou doest good;
teach me thy statutes."

Psalm 119:68

7
Fidelity:
Love as
Persistent Presence

The Harvest of the Spirit

"The Lord is faithful" (2 Thess. 3:3, KJV). This is the theme with which the discussion of faithfulness must begin. So the psalmist says:

> "Where can I escape from thy spirit?
>   Where can I flee from thy presence?
> If I climb up to heaven, thou art there;
> if I make my bed in Sheol, again I find thee.
> If I take my flight to the frontiers of the morning
>   or dwell at the limit of the western sea,
> even there thy hand will meet me
>   and thy right hand will hold me fast."
>   Psalm 139:7-10

The faithfulness of God is like that, and God asks the same faithfulness from us.

Fidelity is love as persistent presence.

For a moment let us move back and forth between these two realities: the faithfulness of God and the faithfulness of Christian love. The steadfast love of God is the one hope which human beings have, for "the Lord is to be trusted, and he will fortify you" (2 Thess. 3:3). At this point love is decidedly not sentimental; it is a tough, concrete, earthy, very tangible attitude and action. It is God's love which stands by us as we forget, fight, envy, hate, and seek only our own interests. It is God's love which stands by as we yawn our disinterest and willfully deny our responsibility to others. It is God's love which overcomes our lack of love and which stands by us even when we are faithless.

This truth requires a pause. Is it not awesome? Mind boggling? Divine charity stands by . . . and stands by. Divine charity reaches out continually, tenderly, forgivingly, renewingly. God is at our side—we who so seldom have really sought to be on God's side.

> *"O Love Divine, what hast thou done!*
> *Th' incarnate God hath died for me!"*
> *Charles Wesley*

The love of God! How can it be? And now the point is drawn, "I give you a new commandment: love one another; as I have loved you" (John 13:34).

The object of our faithfulness makes a difference, for one may faithfully serve an evil or destructive purpose. Blind loyalty can be a terrible slavery. Christian faithfulness is faithfulness to Christ. This is primary; it overrules every other commitment. But Christian faith also means faithfulness to ourselves, to our authentic personhood. To be true to ourselves as transformed by Christ is a necessary quality of Christian living. Finally, Christian faithfulness is faithfulness to our neighbor, to those whom we are privileged to serve. In all of these areas, fidelity is first, acceptance of our responsibility; and second, putting our weight down.

Faithfulness, Evelyn Underhill says, is "consecration in overalls."[1] There is an earthiness about faithfulness, and one of its chief characteristics is sturdiness. It is necessary to stress this, for love has been terribly romanticized. By our romanticism we have set love apart from ordinary life; we have given it a special and separate place.

63

The Harvest of the Spirit

But real love is concrete; it is the most basic ingredient in actual life, in actual relationships. Love is the most essential part of relationships.

A chief characteristic of this love as a part of real life is faithfulness. It is difficult to be faithful in a faithless world, but whatever else love does, it must always be faithful. Love may go beyond faithfulness, but it never goes around it or denies it. In every other expression of love there is a strand: fidelity.

This is true of relationship with God and of relationships among persons. Love pledges its faith to another; that is its persistent way of being love. So we love, "for better, for worse, for richer, for poorer, in sickness and in health." In a recent movie, *Starting Over,* the chief male character says to the woman he loves that he wants to have children with her, he wants to put his teeth in the same glass with hers, he wants to share a gravestone with her. This is a striking, modern affirmation of faithful intention.

Fidelity recognizes the value of the other and expresses this recognition through loyalty. Fidelity is love as strength to endure. It is not a mere disposition to be loyal; it is actually standing by. It is a freely given, generous offer of the self. I am impressed by people who visit nursing homes faithfully—those who go regularly for years, those who continue after illness has altered personality, those who go when recognition has failed. Surely such constancy is a witness to God's unfailing love.

Faithfulness accepts every task for God's sake and is consistent in its devotion to God

*and to the neighbor. Faithfulness serves the
healing of God's creation. Fidelity is love
holding out and holding on.*

Helmut Thielicke has said tersely that the grace of God
does not have "anything to do with larks falling ready
roasted into our mouths."[2] We are not faithful because
everything is going our way. Faithfulness is love in the
moment of testing; it is grace as endurance.

A biographer speaking of John Scott Lidgett, an English
Methodist, says of him: "Absolutely free of the snare of
self-seeking, he filled his mind with the thought of God
and spent his strength in the redemptive service of his
fellow men."[3]

Faithfulness is expressed in many forms. It does not
always take the most publicly recognizable form.
Sometimes circumstances require that it remain quiet and
even hidden, such as in a case where a person takes
meals regularly to another—so regularly that the observer
quickly takes it for granted as a part of the expected
routines of life. At other times, faithfulness is the one
quality which is obvious, as when one stands by a loved
one who is terminally ill, when that is all one can do.
When all other virtues seem to be absent or impossible of
expression, faithful presence is the one gift we can make.
In most cases, fidelity is not showy, just solid.

Clint and Ruth were regular at church. They raised a
family and celebrated a fiftieth wedding anniversary; they
worked hard and tried to learn. But they never taught a
church school class, never said a public prayer, never
made a speech. Their gift was presence. They were
always present and when a job was to be done, a trip to
be made, support for a sick neighbor needed, they were
there. They were faithful.

The Harvest of the Spirit

Faithfulness may persist in chaotic, unstructured situations, or it may be expressed in keeping order among the things committed to our responsibility. What is committed to us? Our relationships—marriage, friendship, parents, children; our jobs—in the home, office, shop, factory, street, car; our neighbors—the poor, the hungry, the sick, the forgotten, the politically disenfranchised. These are our Christian opportunities.

There is a surprising expression of faithfulness in chapter 25 of Matthew. It is startling because the faithfulness which is exhibited is unselfconscious. Perhaps we knew that the unfaithful persons were not aware of their unfaithfulness, but notice the other side. Jesus is commending those who have served him loyally. Some respond by asking, "Lord, when was it that we saw you hungry and fed you?" And Jesus replied, "I tell you this: anything you did for one of my brothers here, however humble, you did for me" (Matt. 25:37,40). Now the point: Faithful service was so much a part of these disciples' lives that they were unaware of the times when they had been faithful!

> *Remember always Jesus,*
> *Who for the joy that was offered him,*
> *Endured the cross*
> *And is forever seated*
> *At God's right hand.*
>
> *AML*

Service to others is the inner ligament of faithfulness. Such constancy is expressed as obstinacy for good causes. Faithfulness stands on the border where personal responsibility moves across to social structure, where individual service is transformed into social order.

66

Faithfulness is loyalty to God and loyalty to other persons. It is always directed outward. Once again, these qualities of the Spirit are not for private possession; they are not jewels kept secretly locked away and brought out only for private admiration. This fruit is not an artificial, cosmetic spirituality; it is not a pious religiosity. Rather the fruit of the Spirit is the most practical, nourishing, shared quality of Christian living.

> *And for such faithfulness there is a final commendation: "Well done, my good and trusty servant! . . . You have proved trustworthy."* *Matthew 25:21*

I once heard a parable. A person visited a fine home and remarked on the beauty of the chandelier in the entrance hall. Later, touring the home, he saw a small bulb at a back stairway. It was unadorned, hardly noticed. But that small bulb prevented more stumbles than the handsome chandelier in the front hall. Such is faithfulness. It does not have to be ostentatious, the first thing noticed, but it must be there, always there, when needed.

The disciples were "not an elite, made up of the outstandingly virtuous, pious, and intelligent; they were the babes to whom the mystery, too simple to be worthy of the attention of the wise and prudent, was given. . . . Their one merit was that they stood with Jesus."[4]

> *Faithful servant,*
> *Enter into my presence*
> *Where the fullness of joy is,*
> *Humble and obedient be,*

The Harvest of the Spirit

My commandments keep,
Every burden put aside,
In my love you shall abide.
I will rejoice and
Set you down by me.

AML

8
Gentleness:
Love as Tender Strength

The Harvest of the Spirit

The word *gentle* historically referred to a person wellborn or a person well-bred. In every case it was descriptive of an actual state of affairs. *Gentleman* or *gentlewoman* referred to a social status; it was not a vague, polite compliment.

Gentleness, as a fruit of the Spirit, is a description of God's relation to us and our consequent way of relating to others. It also refers to a person wellborn and well-bred: our spiritual birth is of a singularly high order (we are the children of God, born of God's mercy into God's family); and we are well-bred, nurtured by the Spirit, coming into full stature in Jesus Christ.

Again we need to stress that the entire harvest of the Spirit is possible because we are in Christ. Christ is the vine; we are the branches; our life and its quality comes from Christ.

Gentleness is near the end of the list of fruits. It is among the last of the harvest, and this is appropriate since the nurturing process extends over a long time. Gentleness requires patient waiting to season; it can never be forced or artifically induced. Yet, when it ripens, it increases the value of life. "How blest," Jesus said, "are those of a gentle spirit" (Matt. 5:5).

Gentleness is softness, but softness of a special kind. There is a softness which comes from controlled strength—softness which describes the athlete or artist who has, through discipline, developed exact control and a soft touch.

> *Gentleness is love which has found how to express its strength in tender ways.*

Gentleness is a quality of spirit which has been transmitted into the physical body. Here both body and spirit interact; here the condition of the spirit finds direct expression in physical characteristics.

The spirit of gentleness expresses an understanding of others which takes their sensitivity into account. The touch of gentleness is the touch of healing; it has discovered the secret of helping with minimum hurt. Such gentleness is characteristic of a good surgeon, an adroit nurse, a spiritual director, or an effective teacher.

Jesus was gentle. We are sometimes uneasy with this quality because we think it is a sign of weakness or that it is an insipid virtue. When we hear the hymn, ''Gentle Jesus, Meek and Mild,'' we may be offended by what we take to be an attribution of negative or recessive qualities to Jesus. But Jesus was gentle; he brought the healing grace of God to hurting human life, and he did it as he actually touched life.

> *So gentleness is known in the concrete*
> *experiences of life. Never isolated, gentleness*
> *is known only in relationships. Life is not*
> *only made attractive by this quality; it is*
> *made useful. "The servant of the Lord must*
> *. . . be gentle."*   *2 Timothy 2:24, KJV*

George Adam Smith, a Scottish biblical scholar of the last century, once said of Dwight Moody, ''Like Luther, he had a very large nature. You require the sea to throw back the full effect of the sun; even the Gospel can attract but feebly when reflected from a small or a narrow man.''[1]

Gentleness indicates a broadness of life. We speak of "gentle, rolling hills" or of "the gentle swell of the waves," and in both cases there is a sense of expanse and gradual undulation. So also in human life, a gentle spirit is one which possesses spaciousness and ability to take time, to range slowly; it provides room for people and time for people to grow and mature and to develop the natural contours of their lives. Gentleness is love as expansive spirit; it is love in its extensive reach. So we pray that we may know "what is the breadth and length and height and depth of the love of Christ" (Eph. 3:18).

Gentleness is a boundless capacity for compassion. It is the opposite of small-heartedness, miserliness of spirit, and rigid tightness. There is in gentleness no acquisitive desire to have all things for oneself. On the contrary, gentleness is the outreach of the inner quality of our being; it is a direct expression of who we are in a basic stance of our lives.

> *"All that will stand and have eternal significance," Colin Morris writes, "are creative acts of compassion—the effectual signs of the presence of the Kingdom."[2]*

In discussing ballet, August Bournonville speaks of the dance finding its summit of talent as "easy grace, in the midst of the most fatiguing movements."[3] So it is that gentleness, which is the ability to lift and lower in easy movement, expresses its character in the most fatiguing and trying moments.

> *Gentleness is firmness with a touch of grace. To be gentle is to know how to touch the*

*place of hurt and convey the sense of
healing; it is the ability to take brokenness in
its arms and adroitly draw the pieces
together through tender force.*

The word *adroit* provides insight, for gentleness is
graceful—grace-filled—movement; it is the movement
which exhibits a continuing smoothness of relation to
another. As in slow motion films, one can watch the
tender touch which conveys agility and strength,
remarkable skill and gracefulness.

The gentleness of which we speak is reflected in our
relation to the natural world. We are to walk softly upon
the earth; to nurture our physical enviroment; to use
wisely its resources; and to help it to be fruitful, to
reseed, and produce fruit once again. Christian life is
expressed in responsiveness to and responsibility for the
earth.

Gentleness should also be expressed in relation to the
social order. The name for gentleness in the political
arena is statesmanship. Gentleness represents the ability
to serve the good over extended time. It is the ability to
insist on the right and to achieve the right in ways which
are constructive and long lasting. It is to change the
present in relation to the long view of what is ultimately
beneficial.

The Epistle of James draws these themes together. "But
the wisdom that is from above is first pure, then
peaceable, gentle, and easy to be intreated, full of mercy
and good fruits" (3:17, KJV). The *New English Bible*
renders the same verse: "But the wisdom from above is
in the first place pure; and then peace-loving,
considerate, and open to reason; it is straightforward and

sincere, rich in mercy and in the kindly deeds that are its fruit.'' And Paul says to the Thessalonians, ''we were gentle among you'' (1 Thess. 2:7, KJV). And so must we be in our world, within our society, and among our neighbors.

The rising sun calls birds
To wake,
To fly,
To meet
Strokes of pink
Brushed upon the morning sky.
                                        AML

9
Self-Control:
Life Shaped by Love

The Harvest of the Spirit

Temperance is an appropriate virtue to conclude the fruits of the Spirit, for temperance brings all of the preceeding qualities to a sharp focus. In the Gospel of John, chapter 15, the fruit referred to is a bunch of grapes. Like an inverted pyramid, temperance is the last grape on the bunch; it is the honed edge of the Christian life.

To understand this, we must look again at the idea of temperance. The verb *to temper* is more appropriate than the noun *temperance,* for to be temperate is to be tempered, brought to a hardness, ready for a cutting edge. Temperance is not a golden mean; it is not the midpoint between extremes; it is not mediocrity or dullness. A temperate life is a life shaped by and directed toward God.

> *Saint Augustine made this interpretation prominent when he said that temperance is love giving itself entirely to that which is loved. He said further, temperance "promises us a kind of integrity and incorruption in the love by which we are united to God."[1]*

To be tempered is to have life clearly directed; it is to have all of our living given shape by the sharp singleness of commitment to God. In a fundamental sense, it is the intemperate love of God which fashions the rest of our affections, actions, and thinking. If we love God with all of our heart and mind and strength, we will love our neighbors as ourselves.

A modern hymn by Jean Untermeyer expresses this understanding.

"Temper my spirit, O Lord,
Keep it long in the fire;
Make it one with the flame, let it share
That upreaching desire.
Grasp it, thyself, O my God;
Swing it straighter and higher!
Temper my spirit, O Lord,
Temper my spirit, O Lord."

Temperance can be illustrated through a metallurgical example. In the production of steel the ore must be melted. But the pure alloy must be tempered for strength. The strength of steel is not only in its hardness, for strength is in part a function of flexibility. Steel that will not bend or give at all will break under stress. Properly tempered steel will yield and bend, but it will not break readily. The measure of elasticity is a part of the strength of the metal.[2] This is the temperance which should characterize Christian life.

Listen again to a previous word, "Every barren branch of mine he cuts away; and every fruiting branch he cleans, to make it more fruitful still. . . . This is my Father's glory, that you may bear fruit in plenty and so be my disciples" (John 15:1-2, 8).

It is the fruit-bearing branch which is pruned; the branch which is capable of bearing fruit is the one that must be cut back. So it is to disciples that this word is spoken. The cost of such discipleship is high, and in our time few of us who call ourselves Christians have begun to accept conscientiously and realistically the challenge of the price.

"The Christian life is always an 'agony,' " says Jacques Ellul, "that is, a final decisive conflict; thus it means that constant and actual presence in our hearts of the two elements of judgment and of grace. But it is this very fact which ensures our liberty. We are free because at every moment in our lives we are both judged and pardoned, and are consequently placed in a new situation." [3] Such struggle creates the possibility of maturity.

> *Free my mind to think on Thee;*
> *Free my hands to do Thy tasks;*
> *Free my feet to walk Thy path;*
> *Free my life for others' sake.*
> *AML*

Maturation works with a disciplining hand. To mature is to go through the discipline of excluding the superfluous and the tangential. In spiritual growth the hand of God and our self-discipline work to exclude and build up. That which detracts is laid aside so that strength may be enhanced.

I am an occasional tomato raiser. There was a lesson in fruitfulness which I had to learn about tomato growing, namely, that to get the best tomatoes you have to "sucker" the plants. The suckers, which are removed, represent new growth capable of producing foliage; they fill out the plant and make it appear bountiful. But they must be removed if the strength of the vine is to feed the fewer but more important fruit-bearing branches.

Jesus said, "You will recognize them by the fruits they bear" (Matt. 7:16). We know a person not only by the fact that he or she bears the fruit of grace, but also by the quality of the fruit which is born. So the writer of Hebrews reminds us, "The Lord disciplines those whom he loves" (12:6).

Christian life is conforming to the will of God.
God acts and we react; we wait passively
before God. But passivity does not mean
inactivity; it means receptivity. We allow God
to form our lives around love.

Maturity requires the sculpting of life by a firm hand.
But how sensitive we are to the touch of this hand. We
are concerned to do so many good things. Our energies
are so diversely directed. We want to be fruitful on every
possible branch, and our strength is dispersed in prodigal
fashion. We live shapeless lives which lack distinctive
features. That which should issue in rich fruiting has only
foliage to show.

> *"He told them this parable: 'A man had a fig-*
> *tree growing in his vineyard; and he came*
> *looking for fruit on it, but found none. So he*
> *said to the vinedresser, "Look here! For the*
> *last three years I have come looking for fruit*
> *on this fig-tree without finding any. Cut it*
> *down. Why should it go on using up the*
> *soil?"'"*
>
> *Luke 13:6-7*

But how difficult it is for us to accept privation. We
want instant sainthood. We want miracle rather than self-
control. At times, walking on water seems easier than
walking on dry ground as a disciple of Jesus Christ.
Some years ago I discovered that the largest contributor
to the United Fund in my university did not own a car,
because, he said, he "could not afford one."

We often want more than we need or more than we can

use in the service of others. An old Yorkshire proverb puts it plainly, "Enough is as good as a feast." Enough for growth and service is enough, and sometimes enough actually provides more strength for service than the diversion of too much.

> *As the culminating fruit of the Spirit, temperance is important, for it makes evident that all of the fruit is grown for a purpose. Fruiting is in the service of love. Consequently, the fruit of the Spirit is directed outward; life has been brought to sharpness for the service of God.*

Self-control is always control for some larger purpose; it is not an end in itself. Discipline is unto God and for God and other persons. We are careful with ourselves so that we may be fruitful for others.

> *The great commandments constitute the Bible's definition of temperance. "'Love the Lord your God with all your heart, with all your soul, with all your mind.' That is the greatest commandment. It comes first. The second is like it: 'Love your neighbor as yourself.' Everything in the Law and the prophets hangs on these two commandments."*
>
> *Matthew 22:37-40*

Such temperance narrows life in order to enrich it. "For the spirit that God gave us is no craven spirit, but one to inspire strength, love, and self-discipline" (2 Tim. 1:7).

Saint Ignatius of Loyola leads us in prayer.

"Take, Lord, all my liberty. Receive my memory, my understanding, and my whole will. Whatever I have and possess thou hast given to me; to thee I restore it wholly, and to thy will I utterly surrender it for thy direction. Give me the love of thee only, with thy grace, and I am rich enough; nor ask I anything beside."[4]

We live in this
Your modest home,
Where stairs are steep
And mirrors few.

Temptation comes to
Be like you,
Take up our cross,
Find comfort in a rose.
                    AML

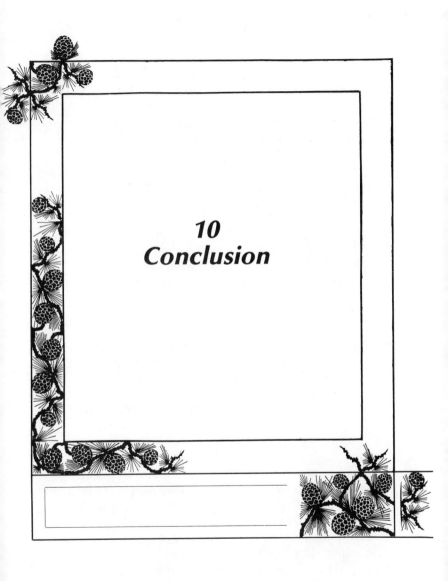

10
Conclusion

The Harvest of the Spirit

*"This is my Father's glory, that you may bear
fruit in plenty and so be my disciples."*
John 15:8

The fruit of the Spirit begins with the gentle thrust of a
tender shoot; the tiny bud of charity breaks the hard and
rigid outline of our lives. The upward movement of sap
which comes from our rootage in God adds new growth
and new shapeliness to our living. Good fruit comes from
a good life. "If the Spirit is the source of our life, let the
Spirit also direct our course" (Gal. 5:25). Jesus warns us
about this:

*"Beware of false prophets, men who come to
you dressed up as sheep while underneath
they are savage wolves. You will recognize
them by the fruits they bear. Can grapes be
picked from briars, or figs from thistles? In the
same way, a good tree always yields good
fruit, and a poor tree bad fruit. A good tree
cannot bear bad fruit, or a poor tree good
fruit. And when a tree does not yield good
fruit it is cut down and burnt. That is why I
say you will recognize them by their fruits."*
Matthew 7:15-20

It is all so simple; it is all so profound. Trees bear fruit
according to their nature. And so do people. Individually
and corporately, persons bear fruit according to their
nature. Christian character is developed around the
worship of God, who is Creator, Redeemer, and
Sustainer. The character of God determines our
character, and the character of God is preeminently
revealed in Jesus Christ.

From deep-rootedness in God our lives grow by nurture of the Holy Spirit. We are drawn into Christlikeness. The bud, the fruit, and the distribution of the fruit are God's work. It is our privilege to have our lives hid with Christ in God and be the supple humanity in which this grace matures.

The psalmist understood this vital living. In the first hymn of Israel, the character of a good person is described:

> *"He is like a tree*
> *planted beside a watercourse,*
> *which yields its fruit in season."*
> *Psalm 1:3*

The vintage season is approaching. The harvest is near at hand. "We pray that you may bear fruit in active goodness of every kind, and grow in the knowledge of God" (Col. 1:10).

Amen.

A Study Guide

General Introduction

A book such as this is most helpful as a point of beginning, when the thoughts of one person give rise to the thoughts of others. Charles Wesley put this idea into two lines of a hymn:

> *"For when the work is done*
> *The work is but begun."*

The important addition you can make will be to relate these fruits to actual life. At each point, think of illustrations in ordinary life settings.

Organization

This guide is prepared to cover six sessions. For each session, every participant is asked to read the designated chapters before the discussion. Perhaps different members can be responsible for special contributions at each session. Let the experience be one of prayer and worship. Begin and end with prayer. Perhaps include a time for singing. Perhaps in each session there can be a discussion of the subtitles—that is, how each fruit is an expression of love.

Session One: Love and Joy
Chapters 1 and 2

Begin with prayer.

A. Love

Discuss love only enough to move into its expressions through the other fruits. We shall end the sessions with an exploration of love as a means of drawing the study to a close, so hold the major discussion until that time.

B. Joy

Which of the descriptions of joy seems most important to you?

What is the range of joy in human life? Can you find illustrations?

How is joy creative?

Read together W. E. Sangster's ten commandments of joy. Have the group comment.

What would you add to the description of joy?

Close with prayer.

Session Two: Peace and Patience, Chapters 3 and 4

Begin with prayer.

In this session, explore and illustrate the dimensions of peace and patience.

A. Peace

Have you learned anything new about peace? What?

How is peace expressed in relationships? In the home? At work? How is peace experienced in the midst of life?

What is the relationship between possessing peace and being a peacemaker?

What is the special quality of the peace that only God can give? Refer to the Washington Gladden hymn, "O Master, Let Me Walk with Thee."

Can you give additional illustrations of the experience of peace in life?

B. Patience

Two words have been used in translation: *patience* and *long-suffering*. Are these two identical? Is *patience* more inclusive than *long-suffering?*

What is the relation of patience to maturity? What are some of the signs of Christian maturity?

How is life paced by God?

How does patience lead us beyond self-interest? Illustrate.

Reflect on John Wesley's covenant prayer. What meanings does this have for you?

Close this session with prayer.

Session Three: Kindness and Goodness
Chapters 5 and 6

Begin with prayer.

Before moving into new material, take the opening minutes to go back and ask if the discussions of joy, peace, and patience have any new meanings for you. Has there been any concrete influence on the way study group members are living? How can such discussion be translated into life?

Both of the virtues before us in this session deal with the basic way we live. We are moving to the core of ordinary life, and we are discussing how ordinary life can be made extraordinary.

A. Kindness

What does it mean to say that kindness is gracious accommodation to others? How does kindness pass beyond self-defensiveness?

Do you think Phyllis McGinley is correct in her description?

What do you make of the statement that the ordinary diaries of our lives are the accounts of our spiritual living?

Can you give illustrations of kind persons?

B. Goodness.

Do you know any good people?

What makes a Christian good? Is it a personal achievement? Does it depend on God's forgiveness? How is forgiveness related to being good?

Discuss goodness and simplicity. What does it mean to say that someone is simply good?

Close this session with each participant, perhaps in silence, setting his or her ambitions for being kind and good.

End the session with prayer.

Session Four: Fidelity and Gentleness
Chapters 7 and 8

Begin with prayer.

Once again we are dealing with exceedingly practical virtues. Make an effort to identify illustrations of how these are present in daily life.

A. Fidelity

Why does fidelity have a touch of earthiness?

In each of these virtues our norm is God's character.
    How is this related to faithfulness?

Read and discuss the passage in chapter 25 of
    Matthew.

What are ways in which we express loyalty to God?

B. Gentleness

In what sense does gentleness require strength?

How is gentleness as a boundless capacity for
    compassion expressed?

Can you describe some gentle people you know?

The statement was made in this chapter that all of
    these virtues come because we are "in Christ."
    What does this phrase of Paul mean? How does it
    underwrite all of our living as Christians?

Close with prayer.

Session Five: Temperance
Chapter 9

Begin with prayer.

Take time in this session to review where you have been as a group. For a few minutes, look back across the virtues already discussed. Are there any further comments about these? Are there any things to be said about incorporating these into personal life? Are there any new discoveries? Is there any fresh harvest?

How do you understand the relation of *to temper*
    and *temperance*?

How does temperance relate to maturity?

Discipline and discipleship come from the same root
word; how do you understand their relationship?
What does pruning mean in Christian experience?
How does focus in life enrich our living?
Close with prayer.

Session Six: Love
Chapter 1 and Conclusion

Open with prayer.

Let us now return to the first chapter. The basic
question is, in the light of the facets we have been
discussing, how may one now give a composite
description of love?

Suggestion: Have each member write a one-page
description of Christian love. Think of love as a
diamond with many facets; how can one capture
in words the glint of light from this jewel? The
group may want to attempt to write a statement
together. Then each person could copy it and take
it as a concrete token of the sessions and as a
resource for further study.

Discuss other books or readings which participants
have found that might be useful for further,
individual study.

For discussion:

What is meant by freedom's embodiment? Read
the fifth chapter of Galatians, especially the
first verses.

Explore the fact that love is never individualistic.

What are some of the meanings in the concluding
poem?

Discuss the prayer in Ephesians 3:14-21.

What are the most important statements in the
conclusion?

Close the session with prayer.

Notes

Notes

Chapter 1

1. H. Richard Niebuhr, *The Purpose of the Church and Its Ministry* (New York: Harper and Brothers, 1956), p. 35.

2. John Wesley, "The Circumcision of the Heart," *The Works of the Reverend John Wesley, A.M.*, vol. 5, *Sermons* (London: Wesleyan-Methodist Book-Room, 1771), Sermon 17, Section 1, paragraph 11, p. 207.

Chapter 2

1. Phillip Schaff, ed., *The Writings against the Manicheans and against the Donatists: A Select Library of the Nicene and Post-Nicene Fathers,* (New York: The Christian Literature Publishing Co., 1886-90), 1st ser., vol. 4, chap. 3, p. 42.

2. Paul Sangster, *Dr. Sangster* (London: The Epworth Press, 1962), pp. 150-51.

Chapter 3

1. James Martineau, *Endeavors After the Christian Life* (London: Longmans, Green, Reader, and Dyer, 1876), p. 50.

2. Karl Rahner, *Foundations of Christian Faith* (New York: Seabury Press, 1978), p. 22.

Chapter 4

1. Margery Williams, *The Velveteen Rabbit* (New York: Avon Books, 1975), pp. 16-17.

2. Hannah Green, *I Never Promised You a*

Rose Garden (New York: Holt, Rhinehart, and Winston, 1964), p. 242-43.

3. Oswald Chambers, *My Utmost for His Highest* (London: Simpkin Marshall, Ltd., 1937), p. 4.

Chapter 5

1. Rita F. Snowden, *The Kindled Flame* (London: The Epworth Press, 1959), p. 90.

2. Flannery O'Connor, *The Habit of Being: Letters of Flannery O'Connor,* ed. Sally Fitzgerald (New York: Farrar, Straus, and Giroux, 1979), pp. 290-91.

3. Phyllis McGinley, *Sixpence in Her Shoe* (New York: Macmillan Publishing, Co., Inc., 1964), p. 226.

4. Dr. Jacob B. Golden in a sermon.

Chapter 6

1. Jane Austen, *Pride and Prejudice* (New York: Modern Library, 1949), p. 185.

2. Dorothy Parker, *The Portable Dorothy Parker* (Middlesex, England: Penguin, 1976), p. 480.

3. Colin Morris, *Get through till Nightfall* (London: Collins, 1979), p. 59.

Chapter 7

1. Evelyn Underhill, *The Fruits of the Spirit* (New York: Longmans, Green & Co., Inc., 1952), p. 27.

2. Helmut Thielicke, *Christ and the Meaning of Life* (New York: Harper & Brothers, 1962), p. 65.

3. Eric W. Baker in *John Scott Lidgett,* ed. R. E. Davies (London: The Epworth Press, 1957), p. 4.

4. C. K. Barrett, *The Signs of an Apostle* (London: The Epworth Press, 1970), p. 28.

Chapter 8

1. Robert C. Mackie, *Layman Extraordinary: John R. Mott, 1865-1955* (Wilton, Conn.: Association Press, 1965), p. 20.

2. Morris, *Get through till Nightfall,* p. 33.

3. Erik Bruhn and Lillian Moore, *Bournonville and Ballet Techniques* (New York: MacMillan, 1961), p. 26.

Chapter 9

1. Schaff, ed., *The Writings Against the Manicheans,* 1st ser., vol. 4, chap. 19, p. 51.

2. William C. Turner, Jr., "The Fruit of the Spirit," mimeographed.

3. Jacques Ellul, *The Presence of the Kingdom* (London: SCM Press, Ltd., 1951), pp. 20-21.

4. Frederick B. Macnutt, comp., *The Prayer Manual* (London: A. R. Mowbray & Co., Ltd., 1961), p. 23.